You Are Weird

Your Body's Peculiar Parts and Funny Functions

Written by
Diane Swanson

Illustrated by
Kathy Boake

KIDS CAN PRESS

Acknowledgments

Standing ovations go to editors Val Wyatt and Stacey Roderick for their ever clever suggestions; illustrator Kathy Boake for her fun, imaginative drawings; designer Julia Naimska for the creative, colorful face she gave the book; and medical expert Dr. Harriet A. Hall, MD, for her review of the manuscript and illustrations. Dr. Hall is a retired family physician/ United States Air Force flight surgeon. She now works as a medical advisor and is a magazine and book author, recently publishing *Women Aren't Supposed to Fly: The Memoirs of a Female Flight Surgeon*.

The British Columbia Arts Council also assisted the making of this book by providing a creative writing grant for which the author is extremely grateful.

Kids Can Press acknowledges the financial support of the Government of Ontario, through the Ontario Media Development Corporation's Ontario Book Initiative; the Ontario Arts Council; the Canada Council for the Arts; and the Government of Canada, through the BPIDP, for our publishing activity.

Published in Canada by
Kids Can Press Ltd.
29 Birch Avenue
Toronto, ON M4V 1E2

Published in the U.S. by
Kids Can Press Ltd.
2250 Military Road
Tonawanda, NY 14150

www.kidscanpress.com

Edited by Valerie Wyatt and Stacey Roderick
Designed by Julia Naimska
Printed and bound in China

The hardcover edition of this book is smyth sewn casebound.
The paperback edition of this book is limp sewn with a drawn-on cover.

CM 09 0 9 8 7 6 5 4 3 2 1
CM PA 09 0 9 8 7 6 5 4 3 2 1

Library and Archives Canada Cataloguing in Publication

Swanson, Diane, 1944–
        You are weird : your body's peculiar parts and funny functions / written by Diane Swanson ; illustrated by Kathy Boake.

ISBN 978-1-55453-282-7 (bound). ISBN 978-1-55453-283-4 (pbk.)

1. Body, Human — Miscellanea — Juvenile literature. 2. Human physiology — Miscellanea — Juvenile literature. 3. Human anatomy — Miscellanea — Juvenile literature. I. Boake, Kathy II. Title.

QP37.S994 2009   j612   C2008-904638-2

Kids Can Press is a *corus*™ Entertainment company

CONTENTS

Odd Bod

Face it. You're weird. You likely have body parts, such as your appendix, that do little more than hang around. You also have parts that simply do odd stuff — such as your skin, which sheds day and night.

There are even parts that make you wonder if they're in the right body, such as the pouch muscles that sit low down in your belly. They're so tiny you aren't aware of them. In fact, about twenty percent of folks don't have any at all. Some have only one, and others — maybe you — have two. Your pouch muscles mainly tug lightly at different muscles in your abdomen. In humans, they don't seem useful at all, but in opossums, for instance, they are large and well developed. Some scientists think these muscles might help support the pouch a mother opossum uses to carry her newborns.

Several body parts — such as your pouch muscles — seem to exist only because you inherited them from your ancestors. They got

DIRECT

them from their ancestors, who got them from theirs, and so on.

Some of your really ancient ancestors lived millions of years ago, so putting ten "greats" in front of the word "grandparents" isn't nearly enough to describe them. Still, many of their body parts were passed on to you —

even if you don't need them. And you might use other inherited parts in different ways than your ancestors did. For instance, they once used their toes for clutching branches, but today you use yours to help you balance and walk on two feet.

Yep, your odd bod is a collection of some very peculiar parts. They show how wonderfully weird you are. Some of them also make you a living museum, providing hints about how your ancient ancestors once lived.

EVOLVING ANIMALS

You're not the only critter who has changed over the generations. The bodies of many animals evolved to suit their environments, and the evidence is in them still.

Whales, for instance, once walked on land as four-legged animals called Ambulocetids. When they moved to the sea, their large legs gradually disappeared. But the bodies of modern whales still contain traces of leg bones.

In some animals, body parts simply changed their jobs instead of disappearing. Did you know that only *female* wasps have stingers? Generations ago, those stingers were used to lay eggs.

Bacteria Bed & Breakfast

Head to foot, you are a bed-and-breakfast hotel for one-celled life forms called bacteria. Oh, sure, you house other microscopic beings, such as fungi and viruses, but you are composed mostly of bacteria. Think of this: approximately ten trillion of the cells that make up your normal, healthy body are human, but another ninety trillion are bacteria!

A few of your body parts, such as your brain, are free of bacteria. But the rest of you hosts hundreds of species. Different body parts provide different environments for different bacteria. Skin, for instance, makes a fairly dry home. It doesn't offer much food variety — mainly skin cells — but it's covered with bacteria. Lucky for you, the species that usually live there crowd out many other microscopic beings that could infect you.

A much richer, moister environment is your mouth. Scientists figure that up to 600 species of bacteria settle there, slurping down saliva and food, such as sugar.

Fewer species live in your stomach. That's not surprising when you consider it oozes acid strong enough to dissolve

Freaky Fact
Right this second, you have more bacteria in your large intestine than the number of human beings that *ever* lived on Earth.

The much slower movement of food through your large intestine makes it a great bed and breakfast for bacteria. Well-fed and comfy, they reproduce quickly there. Some of these bacteria work for you by breaking down really tough bits of food. Some also produce vitamin K, which helps your blood clot when you're cut.

From time to time, the bacteria that live with you might cause problems, but few species do much harm. Just the opposite, in fact. Most pay well for the room and board you provide. And by fighting off other microscopic beings, they may even save your life.

razor blades. Some bacteria escape the acid by tunneling into your stomach's slimy lining. Sounds painful — but you don't feel a thing!

Bacteria that settle in your small intestine have a nutrient-rich home — if they can take the pace. As this long, coiled tube breaks down the food you eat, it pushes the mixture along at a good rate. This works out well for you. The bacteria have less time to feed so more nutrients are left for your body to use.

PASS THE BACTERIA, PLEASE

Shoving extra bacteria into your mouth makes sense to some scientists. They've been experimenting with one species that reduces tooth decay. Added to chewing gum, toothpaste and mouthwash, this species appears to attack bacteria that produce a tooth-eating acid. In fact, the "good" bacteria can knock out 98 percent of the "bad." You still need to brush regularly, though. Your mouth is home to other species of bacteria that can cause tooth decay.

And, by the way, a similar "good" bacteria might be able to fight B.O. Used in deodorants, they could put a stop to bacteria that make armpits smelly.

FLaky BirThday SuiT

In the Charlie Brown comic strip, *Peanuts*, Pigpen is the kid who walks around in a cloud of dust — much like you. Yes, you. Ever since you were born, dead skin cells have been flaking off your "birthday suit" — big time. These cells, plus the skin cells of the people and pets you live with, account for about eighty percent of the dust in your home.

Don't believe it? Do the math. On average, one person sheds about 35 000 dead skin cells every minute. That's more than two million cells an hour … more than fifty million a day. Wow! What a lot of dust.

But don't worry. Some good comes of it. For one, you're feeding dust mites that live in your rugs and pillows.

Er ... if you don't like the sound of that, think about this: the skin cells you shed are constantly being replaced. Every month, you're outfitted with a totally new layer of skin. No wonder your cuts and scrapes heal so fast!

Of all your organs — body parts with special jobs — your skin grows the fastest. It's the biggest, too. Spread out flat, a man's skin could nearly cover a double bed.

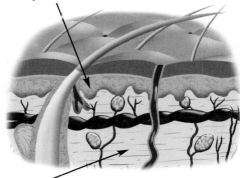

Epidermis

Dermis

Although most of your skin is no thicker than a dime or two, it's made up of two main layers. The outer layer, called the epidermis, is the thinnest. Because it's the layer of skin that sheds, most of its cells work to replace those being lost. The epidermis also gives your skin color. The inner layer, or dermis, helps protect your innards from damage. It also lets your skin stretch when you bend and then reshape itself again. Below the dermis, a layer of fat cells provides insulation that helps control your body's temperature.

Protecting you is your skin's number one job. It prevents many nasty germs from entering your body. It also keeps water from seeping in. And on top of all that, skin holds your insides in and repairs itself when injured. Not bad for something that makes dust bunnies under your bed.

Freaky Fact

An average-sized man sports skin that weighs half as much as a large, 10-pin bowling ball.

CANVAS OF SKIN

For some folks, it's not enough to wear skin. They draw or write on it, too. They make tattoos by injecting ink into the dermis where skin cells don't flake off. That's why a tattoo is permanent, but it shows up well through the thin epidermis.

Most tattoos are decorative, like the leopard-skin pattern on Tom Leppard of Scotland. It covered his body, except for a few places, such as the skin inside his ears.

Other tattoos contain messages. An ancient Greek once wrote a message on the shaved head of his slave. When the hair grew back and hid the tattoo, the slave was sent to deliver the secret message. His head was shaved again so the words could be seen. The tattoo read, "Rebel against Persia."

Leaky Body

Don't look now, but your body is leaking. Water is seeping out all over. Can't see or feel it? Doesn't matter. Even if you're not aware of it, you are always sweating. And sweat is really just salty water.

Every day, you ooze about 0.5 L (1 pt.) of sweat. That's if you're not feeling hot. Drop into a steamy jungle and in a few weeks you could be sweating more than 2 L (4 pt.) an hour — enough liquid to fill half a plastic jug of milk.

Sweat evaporates quickly. The air all around you turns the water in sweat into vapor, which cools you off in the process. That cooling action is sweat's chief task.

However, sweat is good for other things, too. It contains an antibiotic that attacks nasty, disease-causing bacteria that may appear on your skin. On the palms of your hands, it improves your grip — like when you lick your fingers to open a flimsy plastic bag or turn

Sweat gland

the pages of a book. Sweat also softens the skin on your hands so they can feel things easily. (A fine sense of touch would have been especially helpful for your distant ancestors while they picked small nuts and berries to eat.)

As you already know, fast movement makes you sweat intensely. Run several laps around a field and you're soon hot and dripping wet. But have you ever experienced a cold sweat? Extreme fear or worry can cause you to sweat heavily —

especially on the palms of your hands. Just think — that extra sweat might help you get a better grip on the safety bar during a scary roller-coaster ride!

Sweat is produced in coiled tubes, called sweat glands, in the skin's dermis. Ducts link most sweat glands to pores in the epidermis, allowing the sweat to escape. As it evaporates, it usually leaves salt behind. Give your skin a lick and see.

You likely have about two million sweat glands spread over your whole body, except for a few spots such as your lips. But some critters have no sweat glands. For instance, if you were an elephant, you'd have to flap your ears and take mud baths to keep cool. Aren't you glad you leak water instead?

Freaky Fact

Other than a chimpanzee, you have more sweat glands for your size than any other animal.

STICKY SWEAT

Plunk down a dime and press it as hard as you can with one of your fingers. Then lift your finger. See how the dime clings to it for a few seconds? That's because sweat mixes with oil in your skin to make a film that's sticky.

Now scrub your hands well with soap and water, and dry them thoroughly. Press the dime again with your finger. The coin won't cling for long — if at all — because you washed off most of your sticky stuff. See how much time it takes your skin to make enough oil and sweat for your finger to lift the dime again.

Hair Everywhere

There's no arguing that gorillas are hairy beasts. But guess what? You have as many hairs as they do — maybe even more. It's just that theirs are easier to see. Gorilla hairs are thicker and longer than yours. Most of your thin body hairs are only the length of the commas in this book. And these tiny hairs hardly ever grow.

Of course, some of your millions of hairs are obvious. It's easy to see the more than 100 000 strands that cover your head alone. As well, you have no trouble finding your eyebrows, eyelashes and the hairs on your arms and legs. But take a closer look. Except

for places such as your lips, palms and the soles of your feet, you have hairs on every part of your body.

Your hairs do different jobs, depending mostly on where they are. The ones on your scalp, for example, help warm and protect your skull. Eyebrows keep salty water out of your eyes by channeling sweat from your forehead to the sides of your face. Eyelashes help shield your eyes from bright light.

Having hairs everywhere improves your sense of touch. When hairs come into contact with something, nerve endings around the bottom of them send messages to your brain. Test this by touching a few of the hairs on your arm. You won't feel much, but you'll get the idea. Then imagine how well stiff hairs on cats — their whiskers — heighten their sense of touch.

An important use for the thick coats many mammals have is providing warmth. Take the arctic fox, for instance. Its long, thick winter fur — soft hair that grows denser in colder months — helps it survive northern temperatures as low as -60°C (-76°F).

But your thin coat does little to warm you. Hidden under clothing, it doesn't do a whole lot for your sense of

touch either. So why do you have hairs all over you?

Some scientists figure the answer lies with your distant ancestors. They once had thick coats but lost them ages ago. As early people began spending more time away from trees and under the hot sun, they had a greater need to keep cool. Those whose bodies were covered with shorter, thinner hair were more successful and survived. Maybe that explains your skimpy coat.

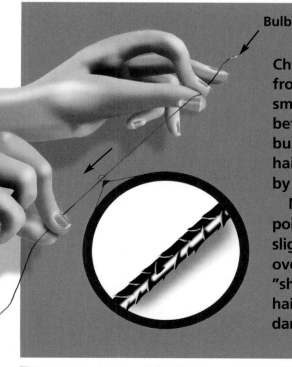

Bulb

COAT CHECK

Check out your coat of hair by yanking a single strand from your head. Examine it closely. The end that has a small bulb on it was in your scalp. Hold the hair tightly between your thumb and pointer finger, just below the bulb. Use your other thumb and pointer to pull along the hair. Do the same thing again, this time holding the hair by the opposite end.

Notice the hair feels smooth when it's pulled from bulb to point. When it's pulled the opposite direction, the hair feels slightly rougher. That's because it has a surface like overlapping roof shingles, and the bottom edges of these "shingles" point toward the tip. This design helps keep your hairs from tangling and makes it easier for dead cells — dandruff — to fall off your skin.

G-g-goose Bumps

You're alone in a dark room, watching a horror movie on TV. Suddenly a slimy monster appears out of nowhere and attacks the hero! You gasp. At the same time, the skin on the back of your neck feels prickly and ... well ... sort of creepy. You're experiencing a galloping case of goose bumps (some folks say "goose pimples" or "goose flesh"). It makes the short hairs on your neck stand on end.

You wouldn't expect your thin skin to have millions of tiny muscles inside it, but it does. That's where muscles that make goose bumps sit. Called erector pili, each muscle is attached to the bottom of a single hair. When these muscles tighten, they create mini-hills — goose bumps — on the surface of your skin. As a result, your hairs stand up.

Goose bumps appear most often on your arms. They can also turn up on your legs

Freaky Fact

Just hearing fingernails scratching across a chalkboard gives some people goose bumps.

and other places, such as the back of your neck. It's possible to get goose bumps on your face, too.

Only mammals, like you, can get goose bumps, so it's odd that they're named after

BUMP BITS

- Yet another word for goose bumps is horripilation (ho-rip-uh-LAY-shun). It comes from two Latin words: *horrere* (to stand on end) and *pilus* (hair).
- Alarm a porcupine and its goose bumps raise sharp, stiff hairs — about 30 000 quills — over much of its body. Not only do the quills make a porcupine appear bigger, but their barbed ends can also pierce what touches them.
- A sea otter can't fluff up its thick fur coat like a fox can because the otter's skin has no erector pili muscles.

excitement, can force the flow of adrenaline — the same hormone that sets your heart racing when you're scared. The adrenaline makes the erector pili muscles contract to form goose bumps and raise hairs. Trapping air beneath them, the hairs hold in some of your body heat.

On animals with thick fur coats, raised hairs hold a lot of air. Fluffed-up coats also make these animals look larger. That's handy if they want to scare something. But goose bumps don't really help you much. Your hairy covering is too thin. Some scientists think that getting goose bumps is simply a reflex you inherited from your hairier ancestors.

a bird. Even doctors use a term for goose bumps that's formed from words meaning skin and goose: *cutis anserina.* Someone somewhere must have thought that the goose bumps on human skin resembled plucked goose skin.

Getting goose bumps is automatic — a reflex action that happens without you thinking about it. Chilly temperatures and strong feelings, such as fear and

Holes in Your Head

It's true! You have holes in your head — and not just the seven you can see. Besides your ears, eyes, nostrils and mouth, you likely have another eight holes in the bones of your skull. They're air-filled spaces called sinuses.

Why they're there, nobody knows for sure. But scientists have a few ideas. One of the most common is that your sinuses lighten the heavy skull that protects your big brain. Given that a full-grown head, minus hair, accounts for about eight percent of body weight, skull-lightening is an important job. When you think about it, how much can a neck be expected to support?

A second idea is that your sinuses work with your nose to warm and moisten the air you breathe. After all, sinuses are connected to the nose by narrow passages. With its thick, moist lining, your nose does a great job of conditioning incoming air on its own, but the linings of your sinuses make the job easier. And it's an important job. Breathing cold, dry air can irritate your nose and throat — and even make your nose bleed.

A third thought is that sinuses help trap germs that can make you sick. The linings of your sinuses, like the lining of your nose, produce a lot of

sticky stuff called mucus. (You might call mucus "snot.") Microscopic hairs in these linings beat back and forth up to 800 times a minute. All that whipping about moves the germ-filled mucus along so you can get rid of it when you blow your nose. The tiny hairs also send some of the mucus to the back of your nose and throat where it is swallowed — yes, swallowed. Then it's up to your stomach juices to attack the germs.

Now meet these amazing holes in your head. There are four different pairs. When you were born, you had only two pairs — the maxillary and ethmoid sinuses — but all your sinuses take years to develop completely.

HORNS MEET HOLES

Your holey head isn't so especially weird. Many other animals have sinuses. In some, such as goats, the frontal sinuses in their foreheads join up with the horns on their heads. But why?

Some scientists figure that this might protect a goat's brain. When courting male goats fight over mates, they can butt heads at speeds up to 60 km (37 mi.) an hour. SMACK! The walls of their sinuses might absorb some of the shock, deflecting it from the brain.

Other scientists have a different idea. They suggest that a goat's frontal sinuses might simply offset the weight of its horns. After all, a lighter skull plus horns is easier on the neck than a heavy skull plus horns.

By the way, some dinosaurs had horns connected to their sinuses, too. Do you suppose what's true for goats might have been true for them?

Name	Location	When Fully Formed	
Maxillary	In your cheeks	About age 12	
Ethmoid	Either side of your upper nose	About age 12	
Frontal*	In your forehead	Late teens	
Sphenoid	Behind your nose	Late teens	

* Some folks have one or none, instead of a pair.

Too Many TeeTh

Sink your teeth into this: most people have jaws with space for just twenty-eight teeth, but another four may try to squeeze in. And since these extra four teeth are usually big, they can mean trouble.

Third molars, as they're sometimes called, are teeth built for grinding and chewing. They start forming in the gums of ten-year-olds in the far back corners of the mouth. Some third molars never burst out of the gums. Those that do rarely appear in someone younger than seventeen.

That's the age when human jawbones are normally full-grown. It's also about the time that people are full-grown — and supposedly getting wiser — so third molars are nicknamed "wisdom teeth."

But being older and wiser isn't what it's cracked up to be if all these teeth don't fit into a person's head. What's worse, third molars often grow in crooked, sideways, backward — even upside down! Besides, whether or not they push their way out of the gums, they can crowd your other teeth, shoving them out of line.

The roots of third molars can cause problems, too, by spreading out in odd directions. Some wrap around nerves in the jawbones or grow into sinuses in the cheeks. That makes the molars

FOUR JAWS FULL

Think you have a lot of teeth? Consider an eel called the reticulated moray (rih-TICK-yuh-LAY-ted MOR-ay). It's a snakelike fish with two pairs of jaws, both lined with teeth. The moray normally keeps its second pair deep inside its throat. Then, when it nabs prey, it fires the second set of jaws and teeth into action. They snap forward to grab the prey from the teeth in the moray's mouth and drag it down the throat. Scientists figure there might be other fish in the moray eel family that have two sets of teeth. But the reticulated moray is the first they've found.

hard to remove, and the roots that grow into sinuses can lead to infections.

Scientists figure that third molars were once much more useful — and less trouble —

than they are now. Early humans chewed more than you do. To get the energy they needed, they ate a lot of roots, leaves, nuts and meat — raw foods that required a lot of grinding before swallowing. They made good use of their third molars by eating these foods. And they had jaws large enough to house broad wisdom teeth.

Modern food is mushier than diets of long ago. And compared to your ancestors, you eat a lot of food that's softened

through cooking. You also use knives and forks instead of depending on teeth alone to break up your meals. No wonder you don't need third molars much. Still, because your ancestors had them, you'll develop some anyway.

Today, many dentists recommend removing wisdom teeth. Face it: these molars aren't much use to us, and they can certainly cause a lot of trouble. Good luck with yours!

Freaky Fact

Elephants get their last and biggest molars when they're about 40 years old. Each of these teeth is more than 30 cm (12 in.) long.

Vampire Fangs

Candles flicker as a man in black sweeps down a winding staircase, his full-length cape flowing behind him. At the bottom, he grabs a beautiful young woman and bares his teeth. She faints as he prepares to drink her blood ...

The long canine teeth of the famous vampire Count Dracula are known around the world. They are sharp and strong — like yours, only longer. Look in the mirror to check yours out. They're the pointiest teeth you have. Sometimes these teeth are called fangs — even on people. But you're no vampire, so what are canine teeth doing in your mouth?

These four strong, pointy teeth help you tear off chunks of solid food, such as apples and steak. With deep roots, they're the longest, most stable teeth you have. Still, they're not nearly as long and stable as the canines of many other animals. Walruses, for instance, have upper canines called tusks that are close to a meter (3 ft.) long. They're so strong they can be used like steel picks, helping the walruses haul themselves from the sea up onto the shore.

Your canines certainly aren't tusks. And you never use them to stab prey like lions do. Nor do you battle with your canines like a wolf fighting for a mate. You don't even bare them to threaten enemies as baboons do. Just the opposite, in fact. You show your canine teeth most when you laugh.

A long time ago, however, your apelike ancestors may have displayed their canines in scary snarls. They might also have used them to fight and to nab prey. But as they developed hands (instead of front feet) and started using tools, they needed their canines less and less. And when they began eating more roots and seeds, their big canines got in the way of side-to-side chewing. Teeth became smaller over the years, just like jaws. So, today, you're left with little Count Dracula fangs.

Freaky Fact

The upper canines of a male warthog often curl upward and may grow to be 25 cm (10 in.) long.

CANINE CLOSE-UP

Wash your hands well, and rub a finger over the gums above your top teeth. Feel the bumps? Those are the roots of your teeth. Notice your canine roots form the biggest bumps? You can feel them even when they're covered by your upper lip. Some people have canine roots long enough to reach their eye sockets. That's why canines are also called eyeteeth.

If you know a friendly dog — one that would let you look at or even feel its teeth and gums — you can discover why canines have another name: dog teeth. A dog has very long canine teeth, including roots. Compared to yours, its teeth are more pointed, too — good for catching prey as its ancestors, the wolves, did. No wonder dogs and wolves are also known as canines.

Eccentric Eyeballs

When Veronica Seider was a university student in Germany during the 1970s, she could recognize faces 2 km (more than a mile) away. That's sharp eyesight for a person — about twenty times keener than average. You could say Veronica's eyes were a bit weird, but so are yours.

For one, there's that arc-shaped fold in the inside corner of each of your eyes. Look for a fold as you peer in a mirror. It's not the pink blob that makes goop or "sand" when you sleep, but the taller, pale-colored tissue behind the pink blob. See it?

No one knows what it's doing there. Some think it might help pass dirt to the blob or help hold the eyeball in place. Still others suggest that it's what is left of a third eyelid — one your ancestors had ages ago and passed on to you.

After all, many animals today have three lids — upper and lower ones, like yours, plus a third that's mostly stored in the eye socket. This third lid moves independently, sliding sideways across the eye. It removes grit and moistens the eyeball by spreading mucus and tears around. Upper and lower lids do this, too, but the third lid does a better job. That's because it's usually clear, so it can stay closed and hold moisture against the eye while still allowing the animal to see.

Sporting a pair of clear, third eyelids is like wearing goggles. They protect the eyes. In the water, they guard crocodile eyes from floating litter. Among tall grasses, they keep prickly seeds out of horse eyes. And in the sky, they shield

Another odd thing about each of your eyes is its blind spot. You see nothing where blood vessels and a major nerve pass through the back of the eyeball. Your eyes have millions of cells that receive images and send on the information to your brain, but there are none — zero — at that point in either eye.

Luckily, though, you have two eyes. Their images overlap, which helps you see what your blind spots miss. Your brain also kicks in, using whatever surrounds the blind spots to "fill in" the images for you. Now that's out of sight!

to do that, they might smash into trees.

So why don't your arc-shaped folds work as third eyelids for you? Maybe you just don't need them as much. Think about it. You don't normally poke your head into water or tall grass to feed. And how often do you soar through the air like an eagle?

eagle eyes from rain and bright light. If eagles had to close their other lids

GO BLIND

Normally you're not aware of your blind spots, but you can find them. Try holding this page at arm's length, and cover your left eye. Stare at the triangle while gradually bringing the book near. See how the rectangle "disappears" when the book reaches your blind spot? You didn't "see" a hole where the rectangle was because your brain filled in the spot, using the rest of the page as a guide.

Now find your other blind spot. Cover your right eye. Stare at the rectangle with your left eye, and move the page closer to see the triangle "disappear."

▲   ■

Ears That Wiggle

Ever watch a cat swivel its ears to detect sound? It has more than thirty muscles in each ear. You can't match that, but you do have a few muscles that can move your ears.

There are three muscles in your scalp around each ear. The largest muscle, just above the ear, raises it. The smallest, in front, pulls the ear forward. The muscle behind draws the ear backward.

A few folks — you may be one of them — can use some of these muscles to make their ears wiggle, but most people can't. They probably don't even know they have ear muscles.

Scientists think your ancient ancestors might have had ears that pointed upward and turned like a cat's. Focusing on the direction a sound came from helped them catch prey and avoid predators. Then, over the ages, their ear muscles got smaller, and the part of the brain that controlled these muscles seemed to shrink. Ears also became

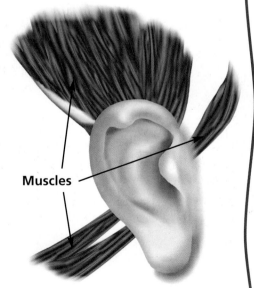

Muscles

MAKING LIKE DOPEY

Remember Dopey in Disney's *Snow White and the Seven Dwarfs*? He was famous for wiggling his big ears. The movie's art director, who could also wiggle his ears, inspired Dopey's unusual skill.

Some people who weren't born with the ability to wiggle their ears actually manage to learn how. They spend hours in front of mirrors making their brains aware of their ear-wiggling muscles. First, they try to sense just where the muscles are by watching their ears twitch as they open and close their mouths. (Ear muscles usually move when other head muscles do.) Then, while they touch the muscles near one ear, they practice moving only those muscles. After people master wiggling one ear, they sometimes try to teach themselves to move both ears at the same time!

more rounded — probably as people hunted less and less for their own food and spent fewer hours directly avoiding predators. A few people today, however, have a bump on the inside of the upper fold of one — or both — of their ears. It may be all that's left of the tip from their pointy-ear days.

But even if you can wiggle your ears, you can't turn them around. You can change the position of your ears by moving your head, though. Having a head between your ears actually helps you pinpoint noise. That's because

sound waves usually reach one ear slightly before they reach the other. In other words, your ears hear in stereo. Each one acts separately to detect sound. Your brain automatically uses the difference in the time that sound reaches each ear to figure out the direction of the noise.

Do you suppose wiggling your ears dislodges much earwax? That's the stuff that forms in your ear canals — the channels that carry sounds into your head. Sticky earwax mixes with oils, sweat and flakes of dead skin. It's gross,

but it traps dirt and helps keep water out of your inner ears. Old wax eventually dries up and falls out.

And before you make a face, think about this: earwax was highly valued by artists years ago. To get rid of bubbles, they mixed it with whipped egg whites in colored glazes.

Freaky Fact

Male ear-wigglers outnumber female ear-wigglers about two to one.

Stereo Sniffer

Take two clean fingers — your pointers will do — and poke them just inside your nostrils. Now press your pointers gently together. Notice the wall between your nostrils is so thin that it barely separates your fingers.

In fact, it's odd that your body even bothers to create two individual nostrils. But there's a reason — you actually sniff in stereo. Your two nostrils act separately to sense one odor.

For a long time, scientists couldn't understand why you didn't simply have one big hole in your nose. Then they discovered that each nostril receives slightly different concentrations of smells at slightly different times. Your brain compares the odors from your two nostrils to figure out where the smell is coming from. It's similar to the way your brain compares sounds that enter each ear and figures out the source (see page 25).

High inside your nose are nerve cells coated with mucus (snot). Odor chemicals from flowers, soup or anything else you sniff drift in through your nostrils and up your nose. There they dissolve in the mucus and excite the nerve cells, sending signals about the smell to your brain.

Each nostril samples odor chemicals from slightly different spots. Scientists estimate the centers of these spots are only about 3.5 cm (1 1/2 in.) apart. But that's enough to help your brain pinpoint the source of a smell.

Millions of years ago, sniffing might have been easier for your ancestors. To dissolve odor chemicals, they likely had moist flesh around their nostrils as well as inside their noses — like a dog's wet nose. And on each side of the divider that separates the nose's two passages was a small pit that also received odors. You still have those tiny pits in your nose, but they no longer work. Don't bother looking for them, though — you won't be able to see them.

As your ancestors started to depend more on their eyesight to make sense of their world, smell became less important and noses changed. Still, the system of sniffing in stereo — as you do — has been working well for years.

SUPER SMELLERS

- Male emperor moths are some of the best sniffers on this planet. They can smell a mate up to 11 km (7 mi.) away. But, unlike you, these moths use antennae to smell.
- With their keen sense of smell, bison can detect predators, such as grizzly bears, and even locate water to drink.
- Police dogs trained to sniff out illegal drugs are actually just searching for toys. They love games of tug-of-war, so their trainers play with them using towels that smell of drugs. The dogs soon link that smell with toys.

Dead-End Tube

ook out! There's a worm inside you. It's about as thick as your thumb and roughly 7.5 cm (3 in.) long. Oh, hang on. That's just your appendix, but it sure *looks* like a worm. That's probably why its full name is vermiform appendix. "Vermiform" means wormlike.

You can press against your appendix by pushing on the lower right side of your belly — but don't expect to feel it. Of all the parts in your body,

it can be the hardest to pin down. Your appendix begins close to the spot where your small and large intestines meet. But where it actually ends varies widely from person to person. It may curl up under the liver, lie beside the kidney or dangle straight down.

Your appendix is simply a tube that's closed off at one end. There's not really much to it. Why you have one is anybody's guess. But some

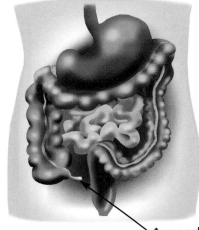

Appendix

scientists think that your distant ancestors once had much larger appendixes than the one you may have. Those larger tubes may have helped them digest huge amounts of plants, including the really tough bits that your body has trouble breaking down.

Over many years, the size of the appendix shrunk. It got smaller as your ancestors adapted to eating different kinds of food, such as meat. Certainly it does nothing to help you digest your meals today.

It might be that your appendix helps you stay healthy by supporting your immune system in fighting

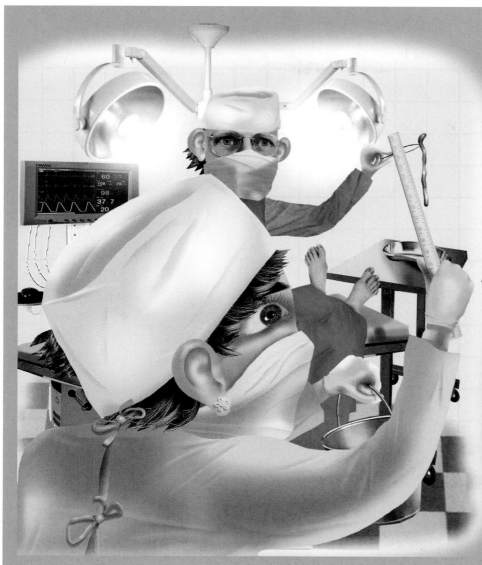

AMAZING APPENDIXES

- In 2006, doctors in Croatia removed one of the longest appendixes ever found in a person. It was more than 26 cm (10 in.) in length. That's likely three times as long as your appendix.

- A rabbit's appendix is longer than that of most other mammals. It averages about 10 cm (4 in.) in length. That's even a good size for a human appendix, and think how much bigger you are than a rabbit. Having a large, well-developed appendix helps a rabbit break down cellulose — the tough part of plants.

off infections. That may have been especially true during your baby years but, oddly enough, the appendix itself can easily become infected — something that could even threaten your life. This can happen when the opening to the appendix gets blocked. Then masses of bacteria take over. Your appendix can burst and spread infection throughout your belly. Arghhh!

Removing an infected appendix doesn't appear to make your immunity any weaker. After all, people born without an appendix seem to have as tough an immune system as anyone else. Go figure.

Freaky FacT

Aulus Celsus, an early Roman who wrote about medicine, discovered the human appendix around 30 AD by dissecting executed prisoners.

Recyclable Muscles

You've probably seen them pumping iron on TV or perching on lifeguard chairs — big, strong dudes, their arms and legs bulging with muscles. It won't amaze you to learn that they have more muscles than they need. But — surprise! — so do you. Believe it or not, your legs and arms likely have muscles you could get along just fine without. Or you might even be one of at least ten percent of folks around

PROBE YOUR PALMARIS

Raise your right hand so your palm is facing you. That's it. Now press your thumb and smallest finger tightly together, and bend your wrist slightly toward your face. The palmaris tendon — if you have one at all — should stand out easily. It's the cord that runs downward from the middle of your wrist.

With your left hand, feel the underside of your right wrist. Notice how loose your palmaris seems. Check with your friends to see if they have palmaris tendons, but don't be too surprised if they don't!

the world who never had them in the first place.

The spare parts in your legs are called plantaris (plan-TAR-iss) muscles. Along with their tendons — cords that attach muscles to bones — they run through the calves of your legs to your heels. They're weak, but they can help you bend your knees and ankles.

The plantaris parts are so long and skinny they often fool first-year medical students into thinking they are nerves. That might explain why plantaris muscles and tendons are sometimes called "fool's nerves."

Your arms may have spare parts, too, called palmaris (paul-MARE-iss) muscles. With their tendons, they run

from the elbow to the wrist. They help you bend your wrists and fingers but, like your extra leg muscles, they are weak.

Many monkeys make good use of all their leg and arm muscles when they travel from tree to tree. Their plantaris parts not only help bend knees and ankles, they also flex toes all at the same time — great for getting a good grip on branches. Palmaris parts in monkeys' arms are strong as well, helping them hang and climb easily.

But you don't spend much time hanging or climbing in trees where you'd really use your arms' palmaris parts. And the plantaris tendons in your calves don't even reach your toes. If you have these

weak arm and leg muscles at all, it's probably because you share ancient ancestors with monkeys — ancestors who moved quickly through forests by swinging from the branches.

However, having a few extra muscles and tendons can be a good thing. Believe it or not, doctors are able to recycle them. They can use sections to fix other moveable body parts, such as thumbs, that aren't working well.

Freaky Fact

While some folks have absolutely no palmaris muscles in their arms, others may have extras.

Tail from The Past

Run your fingers down your lower backbone to the very end. Feel a small bone with a rounded tip? That's your tailbone — all that's left of an actual tail you had before you were born.

A two-month-old human embryo has a well-formed tail. It's tiny, but at the time it's larger than the legs that are also developing. The following month, it starts to shrink. Then it usually disappears.

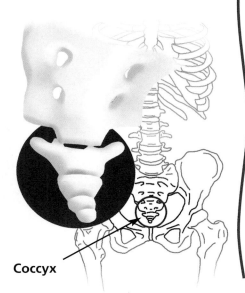

Coccyx

Technically, a tailbone is called a coccyx (KOCK-six) and, at first, it's not a single bone. It's up to five bones growing together. In some people, the bones fuse to become two or three. In others, the bones gradually become one. Either way, a tailbone is usually rigid by the time a person is twenty-five years old.

Now don't think you can ever train your tailbone to wag. Each bone in it is thoroughly solid. That means your spinal cord, which controls your spine's movement, cannot pass through the tailbone the way it does through the other bones of your backbone.

You and your pal likely have very different tailbones, just as you have different heights, weights and hair colors. Your buddy's tailbone may be bigger or smaller than yours, but it's somewhere between 3 and 10 cm (1 and 4 in.) long. And while your friend may have a tailbone that curves, yours might point straight forward or straight down.

A tailbone can make a useful hitching post for some of the body's muscles, but these muscles could be — and occasionally are — attached to other bones instead. In fact, there are people who have no tailbones at all, and their muscles are just fine without them.

Unlike you, your ancient ancestors had tails that were highly developed. They might have used them as fifth limbs — much like many monkeys do when they swing through forests, grabbing branches with their tails as well as their other limbs. If your ancestors had tails as nimble as these, they may have also used them to nab and hold food while they ate. Your ancestry probably explains why you have a tailbone today — and that's no tall tale.

Freaky FacT

No European would have wanted to be born with a tail between the years 500 and 1000 AD. Both child and mother were believed to be witches and were put to death.

TAIL TALES

- Even though a few babies arrive with a tail, doctors today usually remove it at once. In centuries past, however, some human beings lived with tails up to 15 cm (6 in.) long. In 1889, the magazine *Scientific American* described an extra-long tail on a 12-year-old boy from Thailand. It measured nearly 30 cm (12 in.).
- Coccyx comes from the Greek word *kokkyx*, meaning cuckoo bird. Some folks think that's because a human coccyx resembles a cuckoo's beak. Others suggest it's because a cuckoo's call sounds like ... ahem ... farting, which happens close to the human coccyx. To support this idea, they point to an old name for the coccyx: whistle-bone.

CLaWS!

Got an itch? Scratch it. Knot in your shoelaces? Pick it apart. Fingernails are handy tools that you've always had — even before you were born. But, long ago, having nails was more important than it is now. They were the best scrapers and tweezers around. Your ancient ancestors used them often in everyday chores, such as plucking lice from their hair and opening nuts to eat.

Much farther back in time, your ancestors' ancestors had narrow, curving claws instead of wide, flat nails. The claws were thick and strong, especially good for fighting or for catching prey and ripping it apart. Animals such as tigers and eagles use theirs the same way. But having claws wouldn't help you much nowadays. When you tried to twirl spaghetti on a fork or turn the pages of a book, they'd just get in the way. So it's a good thing your ancestors' claws broadened and flattened, changing to nails over time.

Not surprisingly, both claws and nails are made of the same tough stuff: keratin. It's a protein that resists tearing and breaking. Without keratin protection, the ends of your fingers and toes could easily

be injured. If you've ever cut a nail too short, you know how tender an unprotected digit can be.

The cells in nails and claws are already dead, but these

hard endings grow from living cells. As new cells form in the skin, they push the old dead cells — containing keratin — out over the digits to become protective nails and claws.

Of course, dead cells have no feeling. That's why it doesn't hurt to cut your nails. But removing whole nails from the living cells in the skin hurts a lot.

While having your live digits end in dead cells may sound bizarre, it seems even odder that humpback whales grow keratin "nails," called baleen, from their mouth skin. The humpbacks use baleen to strain food floating in the water. So as weird as you are, isn't it nice to know that you have company?

FINGERNAILS: THE UNCUT STORY

If you've been avoiding the nail clippers, think of Shridhar Chillal of India. He heard of a Chinese saint who grew long nails, so he figured he'd try that, too. When he was fifteen, Shridhar refused to cut the nails on his left hand. He used only his right hand for chores.

He also trained himself to sleep lightly so he wouldn't accidentally roll on his ever-growing nails.

Forty-eight years later, Shridhar's fingernails were long and twisty. They weighed so much that they permanently damaged his left hand. Still, Shridhar's nails had made him different, even famous. When he finally cut them in the year 2000, their combined length was more than 6 m (20 ft.)!

Extra Toes

When people are only 2.5 cm (1 in.) long — just eight-week-old embryos — their toes are already forming. As they grow, they likely discover that toes are handy things to suck, both before and after birth.

Later they will find other uses for toes, just like you have. These digits make you taller and quieter as you tiptoe across the floor. And by scrunching them up, they keep your flip-flops on.

The big, or first, toe is the most important one. It helps you keep your balance. It also works as a lever, pushing off the ground with every step you take. Without it, moving on two feet would be hard, if not impossible, to do.

Now what about the rest of your toes, especially the smallest — your baby toes? While toes two, three and four seem to help your big toes, those fifth ones don't appear to do much. You certainly don't need them to walk. On some people, baby toes do not even touch the ground. And people who have lost them in accidents or to diseases still get around fine.

You probably have ten toes because your ancient ancestors did. At one time, they spent a lot of time in trees where they used their feet like hands and their toes like fingers. All four "hands" and twenty "fingers" worked together to grip branches. It made climbing and hanging in trees easier.

But your ancestors slowly evolved. They began walking more often than climbing, so their bottom pair of "hands" changed to look and act like feet. The "fingers" became toes, gradually shortening for easier movement on the ground. Further, the digits that were "thumbs" shifted

position. They moved closer to the other toes where, as big toes, they would be more useful for walking.

Despite all this, you hear about people who can do amazing things with their toes. For instance, folks born without hands have trained their toes to type on keyboards or to paint pictures. So your toes may be capable of doing more than you think. Ever tried holding a pencil between your first and second toes to see if you can write your name?

Freaky Fact

Bison are big animals, but they move like ballerinas — on their tiptoes. Wrapped in a tough coating, each hoof is really the tips of two toes.

BIG TOE FOR MUMMY

Who would have thought it? Ancient Egyptians made artificial toes. One false big toe that researchers found was still attached to the foot of a mummy in a tomb. The mummy had been a 50- to 60-year-old woman who probably lost her original big toe through disease.

Made of wood and leather, the false toe is up to 3000 years old. It was likely sturdier than at least one other ancient false toe found in Egypt. That one consisted of linen, glue and plaster. But both toes show signs of wear, so it seems they were actually used for walking — not just for looks.

Unsolved Mysteries

If you like mysteries, take a good look at your own weird self. There's a bundle of puzzles within your body. What exactly do your sinuses do? When are ear muscles useful — if ever?

Why are there arc-shaped folds in the corners of your eyes? How does body hair help you … or does it?

These are only a few of the questions you might be wondering about. Scientists wonder about them, too. They're trying to find some answers as they peer through microscopes, piece together ancient skeletons and examine living bodies.

If you could count all your ribs, you'd likely find twelve pairs. Forming a "cage" of sorts, they protect the organs in your chest. But you might be one of the eight percent of folks who have an extra rib or two. Or, just as weirdly, you might have been born with only eleven pairs of ribs. Why do some people have fewer ribs and others have some to spare? Nobody knows.

And what about those sudden jerks you sometimes feel just as you're falling asleep? Could they be leftovers from the days — and nights — of your ancient ancestors? Perhaps they were the defensive moves of nerves and muscles that woke up your ancestors to keep them from falling off tree limbs where they slept.

Scientists make many educated guesses about why you operate the way you do. But some of their ideas have yet to be proven. Like you, they are struggling to figure things out. What's more, some of what they learn will likely change over time. That's the nature of science. New discoveries bring new information, which generates more ideas about how the human body works.

So stay tuned for future announcements. Even better, become a scientist yourself one day and join the investigation. There are many mysteries to solve before anyone can explain just why you are so weird.

GLossary

adrenaline: a hormone that increases heart and lung action

ancestors: family members, such as great-great-great-grandmothers, who lived long ago

appendix: a small tube attached to the large intestine

bacteria: microscopic one-celled life forms

canine teeth: four sharp, pointed teeth, each sitting between front teeth and molars

cells: the smallest functioning units of life forms

coccyx: the tailbone at the bottom of the backbone

dermis: the thicker, inner layer of skin

embryo: an unborn life in its first eight weeks

epidermis: the thinner, outer layer of skin

erector pili muscles: tiny muscles attached to the base of hairs in the skin

germs: microscopic life forms that may cause diseases

glands: groups of cells that produce liquids the body needs

hormone: a substance made by the body and delivered to an organ by the blood

immune system: parts of the body that fight infection, disease and poison

keratin: the tough protein in hair, nails, feathers, horns and hooves

large intestine: a digestive organ that joins the small intestine and the anus

molars: back teeth with flat tops for grinding food

mucus: slime that moistens parts of the body and protects them by trapping germs

nerves: long fibers that carry messages between the brain and other parts of the body

organs: groups of cells, such as eyes, ears or skin, that do a particular job

palmaris muscles: arm muscles that might help bend wrists and fingers

plantaris muscles: leg muscles that might help bend knees and ankles

sinuses: small holes in the skull

small intestine: a digestive organ that joins the stomach and the large intestine

species: in most cases, a type of life form that breeds and produces young that can reproduce

spinal cord: a thick cord of nerves enclosed in the backbone

tendons: strong cords that attach muscles to bones

Index